CASEY JONES

Library of Congress Number: 87-4600

Library of Congress Cataloging in Publication Data

Gleiter, Jan, 1947-
  Casey Jones.

  (Raintree stories)
  Summary: The life of the railroad engineer, famous
for always bringing his train in on time, and whose
last ride on the Cannonball Express inspired the
well-known ballad.
  1. Jones, Casey, 1863-1900—Juvenile literature.
2. Locomotive engineers—United States—Biography—
Juvenile literature. [1. Jones, Casey, 1863-1900.
2. Locomotive engineers] I. Thompson, Kathleen,
1944-   II. Balistreri, Francis, ill. III. Title.
TF140.J6G43   1987   363.1′22′0924 [B] [92]   87-4600
ISBN 0-8172-2653-2 (lib. bdg.)
ISBN 0-8172-2657-5 (softcover)

CASEY JONES

Jan Gleiter and Kathleen Thompson

Illustrated by Francis Balistreri

Raintree Childrens Books
Milwaukee

"Come all you rounders if you want to hear
A story about a brave engineer.
Casey Jones, that was the rounder's name.
On a heavy eight-wheeler he rode to fame."

It was a man named Wallace Saunders who first sang the song
About a brave engineer and a train gone wrong.

Casey worked with Wallace in the railroad game.
Wallace worked the roundhouse, Casey drove the
train.
It was the first year of the century (or the last year of
the last).
The trains were moving everywhere. The trains were
moving fast.

And then one night in Memphis, Casey brought one in.
It was the "Cannonball Express" and it was heading out again.
The station boss grabbed Casey and he started to explain.
An engineer was sick. Could Casey drive the train?

Casey took a look around the platform where he stood.
He wondered if he ought to and he wondered if he could.
The passengers were waiting underneath the station light.
And there was just one way the train would leave from Memphis that night.

W ell, Casey had been driving hard as any driver can,
But Casey Jones was born to be a railroad man.
He nodded to the station boss and stepped back on
   the stair.
The passengers got on the train and gave the man
   their fare.

They left the station late and headed out into the
    dark.
The Simmons' hound heard Casey's train and ran
    outside to bark.
There were clouds across the moon that night and
    clouds across the stars,
And clouds of smoke above the engine and the
    railroad cars.

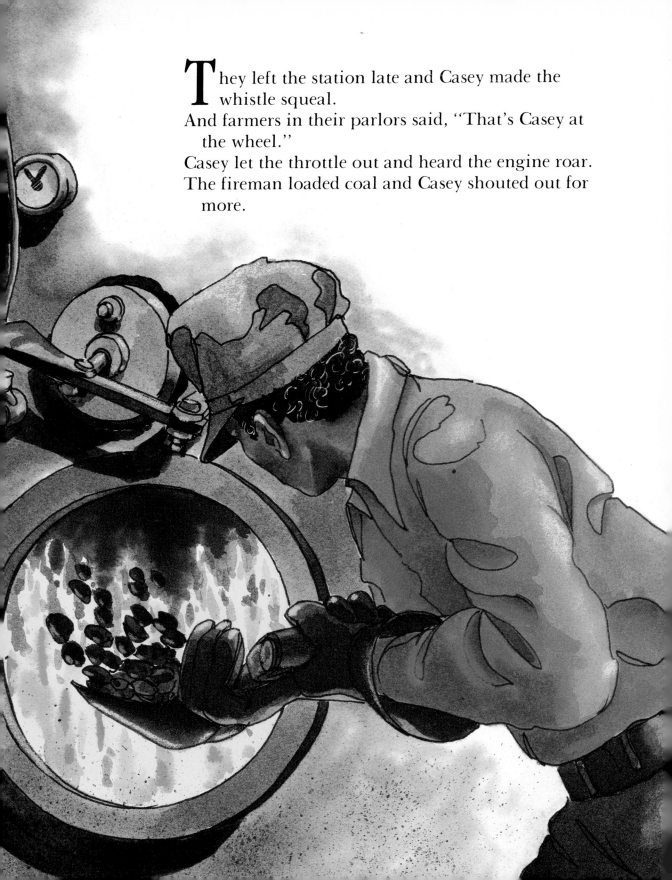

They left the station late and Casey made the
    whistle squeal.
And farmers in their parlors said, "That's Casey at
    the wheel."
Casey let the throttle out and heard the engine roar.
The fireman loaded coal and Casey shouted out for
    more.

They went across a mountain and they went
around a bend.
They went through Tennessee and they were moving
like the wind.
They got to Mississippi at the tail end of the night.
Then Casey saw a shadow in the morning light.

He saw the shadow as he came like thunder down a
    hill.
The shadow was a freight train and the train was
    standing still.

The freight train shouldn't have been there. The track should have been clear.
The Cannonball couldn't stop in time. And Casey Jones knew fear.

But Casey never hesitated. Too much was at stake.
One hand went for the whistle, and the other for
the brake.
He yelled for Sim the fireman to jump, but Jones
stood fast.
He had to try to slow the train until the very last.

Casey was a railroad man. He may have wondered why.
But he had to slow the train or all the passengers would die.

Though Casey lost his life that morning, flags and
    banners waved.
Because of Casey's courage, every passenger was
    saved.

Oh, many cried when Casey died, that fearless
  engineer.
And one man sang a song for all the countryside to
  hear,
About a man, a railroad man up to the very end.
His name was Wallace Saunders, and he sang about a
  friend.

"*All the switchmen knew by the engine's moan*
That the man at the throttle was Casey Jones."